Dinosaurs

KINGFISHER
NEW YORK

KINGFISHER
LONDON & NEW YORK

Published in the United States by Kingfisher,
175 Fifth Ave., New York, NY 10010
Kingfisher is an imprint of Macmillan Children's Books, London.

Consultant: Dr Darren Naish

Designed and created by Basher www.basherbooks.com
Text written by Dan Green

Dedicated to Ellen and Tommy Southgate

Distributed in the U.S. and Canada by Macmillan,
175 Fifth Ave., New York, NY 10010

Library of Congress Cataloging-in-Publication data has been applied for.

ISBN: 978-0-7534-6824-1

Kingfisher books are available for special promotions and premiums.
For details contact: Special Markets Department, Macmillan, 175 Fifth Ave.,
New York, NY 10010.

For more information, please visit www.kingfisherbooks.com

Printed in China
9 8 7 6 5 4 3 2 1
1TR/0512/AYL/WKT/140MA

CONTENTS

Introduction
Dinosaurs

The world has seen *nothing* like the dinosaurs. From terrifying T. rex to massive Argentinosaurus, these stupendous ancient beasts thrived for 160 million years—the largest animals ever to have lived. A man named Richard Owen (1804–1892) gave dinosaurs their name. Literally, it means "terrible lizard." Really? Prehistoric giants? Ever feel like someone is pulling your leg?

Well, think again! It may bust your brain box, but there is hard evidence for the things we know about dinosaurs. Scientists called paleontologists find dino bones in rocks that are millions of years old. These remains give clues to an animal's lifestyle: teeth that shred leaves look very different to those that bite chunks of flesh or crack open shells. Hips tell us which group of dinosaurs a skeleton fits into: saurischians (so-ris-kee-ans) with "lizard hips" or ornithiscians (orn-ee-thisk-ee-ans) with "bird hips." It's taken well over a hundred years to figure out that our planet is always changing, and as it does, life evolves and adapts to the new conditions. Get ready—you're about to see some of the most weird—but real—creatures!

Paleontologists

Chapter 1
Veggie Munchers

Size, when you're a plant eater, really matters! You haven't met the Meat Crunchers yet, but you will soon see that they are not a nice bunch. Sure, some of the Veggie Munchers were blessed with spiked tails and armored plates, but not all of them. Often their only other defense was to pack on the pounds. Boy, did these guys gulp the greens! They were a gassy bunch, too. Well, imagine: tough Jurassic plant matter, eaten in vast quantities, digested in gigantic potbellies filled with super-strong acid. Mmm, if you're still interested in meeting this group, you'd better stay downwind!

Iguanodon

Brachiosaurus

Maiasaura

Triceratops

Stegosaurus

Parasaurolophus

Ankylosaurus

Pachyceph-
alosaurus

Diplodocus

Argentinosaurus

Iguanodon
■ Veggie Munchers

☀ A herding herbivore with a handy set of back gnashers
☀ Had a "fifth finger" on each forelimb for grasping vegetation
☀ This plant lover inhabited most of Europe

I am a dino diva—literally one of the very first dinosaurs
to be named (gooo me!). My skeletons have been found
all over Europe and have given scientists plenty to think
about when it comes to my appearance and lifestyle.

A strict vegetarian, my toothless beak has an overbite
that is very handy for cropping tough foliage. I like to
chew well and have perfected the art of slice-'n'-dice
feeding. Using around one hundred tightly packed back
teeth, I literally shred my food to pieces before swallowing.
Hooves on my forelimbs show that I walk on all fours, but
I can stand on two limbs to feed from high branches.
Like all plant eaters, I'm easy prey but, behold, a secret
weapon: spiked thumbs that are perfect for jabbing at
bullies. Not exactly the thumbs-up a predator looks for!

● Discovered: 1822 (U.K.)
● Pronounced: ig-wan-oh-don
● Name means: iguana tooth

● Period: Early Cretaceous
● Lived: 126–125 million years ago
● Size: up to 33 ft. (10m) long; 5.5 tons

Iguanodon

Brachiosaurus
■ Veggie Munchers

☀ A dino with a small head, a short tail, and a long, long neck
☀ Reached plants that no others could . . . and ate them all!
☀ This biggie lived exclusively in North America

I'm no great risk taker, but I do like to stick my neck out once in a while. Just look at it—towering a ludicrous 30 ft. (9m) above my body, it's not as if I have much choice!

Scientists believe I must have a huge heart to pump blood all the way up. What can I say? I'm a bighearted kinda guy! Just as well, 'cause I'm not big on brains—with a neck this long, the last thing you need is a heavy head to support. With front legs that are longer than my back legs and a short tail, I'm a highbrowser, able to reach foliage at great heights for my nourishment. Of course, I can swing low to eat, too . . . if I want to. My fossils have left scientists guessing at my size, but at more than a ton every three feet (1m), I have to eat like there's no tomorrow. You gotta love the green stuff, I can tell you!

● Discovered: 1900 (Colorado)
● Pronounced: brak-ee-oh-sore-us
● Name means: arm lizard

● Period: Late Jurassic
● Lived: 154–153 million years ago
● Size: up to 75 ft. (23m) long; 44 tons

Brachiosaurus

Maiasaura
■ Veggie Munchers

✳ This maternal duck-billed beast walked on two legs or four
✳ A social animal that laid its eggs in communal nesting sites
✳ Thought to have inhabited only North America

Hello, my dear, you can call me Ducky! I tend to hang out with my own kind, so it's very important for me to get along with folks. Sometimes there are thousands of us in a single herd—handy for keeping Meat Crunchers at bay!

My duck-billed sisters and I make our nests beside one another in a huge nursery. What better way to create a nurturing environment in which to raise the little ones and keep them safe from harm? I take great care of my eggs, covering them with rotten plants to make sure they stay hidden and warm. Like my veggie-munching cousin Iguanodon, I have no front teeth, but my back teeth are arranged in batteries (that's lots of them jammed in tight) for slicing and dicing. Whenever one tooth wears out, a fresh one is always primed, ready to go. Chomp!

- Discovered: 1978 (Montana)
- Pronounced: mah-ee-sore-ah
- Name means: good mother lizard
- Period: Late Cretaceous
- Lived: 74 million years ago
- Size: up to 30 ft. (9m) long; 2.8 tons

Maiasaura

Triceratops
■ Veggie Munchers

✳ A bulldozer with a super-large skull
✳ Safe from most predators once grown to full size
✳ A common beast, yet inhabited only North America

I'm a rootin' tootin' good old boy. I have a barrel belly and a bad temper to boot. I don't wish harm to others; I just don't dig hassle. I'm a six-ton juggernaut and I'll stand my ground. And if there's any doubt . . . I'll charge!

Hey, I'm no looker, but my half-ton head certainly catches the eye. With three huge horns and a frill that's six times thicker than a human skull, woe betide anything that encounters my business end. The frill shields the vulnerable parts of my neck, but I also use it to flash and wink at pretty young things. I spend my time roaming the plains and forests, cropping vegetation with my bony beak. Many of my fossils bear evidence of fierce encounters with power-crazy Tyrannosaurus rex, but healed scars on my frill show that I don't give up easily.

- Discovered: 1887 (Colorado)
- Pronounced: tri-sair-uh-tops
- Name means: three-horned face
- Period: Late Cretaceous
- Lived: 68–65 million years ago
- Size: up to 30 ft. (9m) long; 6.6 tons

Triceratops

Stegosaurus
■ Veggie Munchers

✸ Bus-sized dino with bony plates on its back
✸ This heavy-metal Jurassic giant was well protected
✸ Inhabited western North America and Europe

Talk about armor—I've got hip guards, neck studs, and 17 pairs of diamond-shaped bony plates running down my back. These deter the baddies, while the wicked spikes on my tail deal with those silly enough to strike.

Swung from side to side, my thagomizer (that's my spiked tail) pulverizes anything that tries to sneak up on me or get around my rear end. Ouch! It's no surprise that most Meat Crunchers leave me alone once I'm fully grown. Although used mostly for display, scientists think my plates may also have played a secondary role in temperature control. Sounds wacky, eh? The idea is that the honeycomb of blood vessels pumps blood into the plates to help me cool off when I'm hot and bothered or to absorb heat when I'm feeling chilly. *Brrr!*

● Discovered: 1877 (Colorado)
● Pronounced: steg-oh-sore-us
● Name means: roof lizard

● Period: Late Jurassic
● Lived: 155–150 million years ago
● Size: up to 30 ft. (9m) long; 4.4 tons

Stegosaurus

Parasaurolophus
■ Veggie Munchers

✳ Smooth soul brother with a built-in horn and a big brain
✳ A slow-chewing plant grinder who lived as part of a herd
✳ This crest-headed wonder inhabited North America

I'm a cool cat, man, a totally groovy jazz-o-saurus. That's right, my friend—my schnoz honks. My nasal cavity doubles back on itself inside the 5.9-ft. (1.8-m), backward-pointing crest that sits right on top of my noodle. C'mon, don't pretend you haven't seen it!

My amazing snout is connected to my throat, and when I make a sound, it resonates in the bone chambers like a super-low-frequency foghorn. I can communicate over long distances, keeping the herd together or barking out alarm calls to warn of danger. Like my bug-eyed pal Iguanodon, I move around on all fours but rear up on two legs for noshing on high branches. I have four batteries of rear gnashers—around 800 teeth in total. Locked tight together, they form a single foliage-grinding megatooth.

● Discovered: 1922 (Alberta, Canada)
● Pronounced: pa-ra-sore-ol-uh-fus
● Name means: near-crested lizard
● Period: Late Cretaceous
● Lived: 76.5–73 million years ago
● Size: up to 36 ft. (11m) long; 2.8 tons

Parasaurolophus

19

Ankylosaurus
■ Veggie Munchers

✳ A slow-moving, blundering herbivore that liked to be alone
✳ Despite its armor, no complete skeleton has been found
✳ This thick-skinned dino inhabited western North America

I move around on stout legs, keeping my head low as I chomp on grasses and shrubs. But I'm one big bully, bristling with armored plates and knobs of bone. A massive club sits at the end of my chunky tail. With huge muscles to sweep it from side to side, it pounds and pummels attackers, breaking bones with each swing. Predators, beware!

Ankylosaurus

● Discovered: 1908 (Montana)
● Pronounced: an-kie-loh-sore-us
● Name means: fused lizard

● Period: Late Cretaceous
● Lived: 66.5–65.5 million years ago
● Size: up to 23 ft. (7m) long; 6.6 tons

Pachycephalosaurus

Veggie Munchers ■

❊ Dome-headed dinosaur and potential headbutter
❊ Enjoyed a mixed diet of leaves, seeds, and fruit
❊ Thick skull fossils have been found only in North America

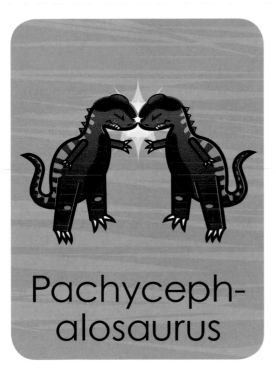

Pachyceph-alosaurus

Hey! You wouldn't wanna crack heads with me, I can tell you. Donk! See, no pain. Thwack! No dizziness. My head is capped with a 10-in. (25-cm)- thick bony dome (leaving precious little room for a brain). I also sport some pretty rad nose cones and spikes around the back of my neck. I run on two legs and use my sharp nipping teeth to tear and taste all sorts of veggie treats. Yum!

● Discovered: 1859 (Montana)
● Pronounced: pack-ee-sef-uh-lo-sore-us
● Name means: thick-headed lizard
● Period: Late Cretaceous
● Lived: 70–65.5 million years ago
● Size: up to 15 ft. (4.5m) long; 0.5 tons

Diplodocus
■ Veggie Munchers

✳ The longest dinosaur known from a complete skeleton
✳ Recently found to have had a row of spines down its back
✳ A peg-toothed dino that inhabited North America

Hey, brother! If you want to walk with dinosaurs, join my laid-back veggie-munching crew. When you get this long, there's not much that troubles you besides finding food . . . if you happen to gobble a ton of plants a day!

My impressively long neck is handy for poking around low branches and shrubs. I just love a tasty fern, and I will bulldoze swathes of forest to get to it. I have been known to topple trees with my tremendous bulk! Visually, my neck is elegantly counterbalanced by my equally long bullwhip tail. Packed with muscle, I can power the tip to swat at unwanted guests. Jurassic veggies have their merits, but in the quantities I get through, it's not all rosy. Bacteria in my gut break down and ferment the food, producing gloriously stinky farts! Just imagine . . .

- Discovered: 1877 (Colorado)
- Pronounced: di-plod-oh-kus
- Name means: double beam
- Period: Late Jurassic
- Lived: 154–150 million years ago
- Size: up to 85 ft. (26m) long; 13 tons

Diplodocus

Argentinosaurus
■ Veggie Munchers

✳ This chunky dino is one of the largest ever discovered
✳ A monster plant eater supported by enormous bones
✳ Not many bones of this beast have been discovered

Ka-*boom*! I'm the South American super heavyweight, one of the largest land animals that Earth has ever known. As an adult, I stand as tall as a five-story building and as long as three school buses. My footprints alone can be deathtraps for smaller animals.

Possibly the heaviest dinosaur of all time, I'm 45 tons meat, 18 tons fat, 12 tons bone, 4 tons blood, and almost 4 tons hide. Wowzer! Baby Argies weigh only a few pounds, which means they need to do some serious gobbling of their greens to grow to my great size (it'll take 'em about 40 years). Good thing our teeth are well adapted for a lifetime of guzzling—there's simply no time to chew when you have to pack on the pounds. These little nippers can strip a branch of foliage in one sweep!

● Discovered: 1993 (Argentina)
● Pronounced: ar-jen-tee-no-sore-us
● Name means: Argentina lizard
● Period: Late Cretaceous
● Lived: 95 million years ago
● Size: up to 98 ft. (30m) long; 83 tons

Argentinosaurus

Chapter 2
Meat Crunchers

Everybody loves a bad guy, and these nasties are no exception. Clawed and jawed, with feathered or scaly skin and mouths brimming with pointy teeth, they have a reputation for violence that is every bit as scary today as it was 100 million years ago. Outnumbered by the Veggie Munchers, the Meat Crunchers left an *impression* nonetheless, evolving in tandem with their veggie prey. For every massive plant lover there was also a giant meat shredder. Several of these beasts hunted in packs, and some of them were pretty fast. So you'd better watch out for what's hiding in the bushes as you step this way . . .

Coelophysis
■ Meat Crunchers

☀ This small fry was one of the first theropod dinosaurs
☀ May have hunted in packs to prey on larger beasts
☀ A little guy that has been found all over the world

Lithe and speedy, I am a runt compared to the monster meat-shredding dinos that followed me. But what does size matter when you're an evolutionary marvel?

That's right! I have a nice pair of slinky lizard hips that allow my legs to drop directly beneath my body. With this solid support, I can stand more upright than many of the creatures from the previous 30 million years. Just watch me scamper around on two legs while using my strong front limbs to grab things. What's that? Anyone can do it? Well, that's easy for you to say 210 million years later, but it was totally revolutionary in my day. And what's more, my skull has large windows in it and the bones of my limbs are hollow, keeping me lightweight and nimble. And you? Mmm, not so smart now, eh?

● Discovered: 1881 (New Mexico)
● Pronunciation: seel-oh-fie-sis
● Name means: hollow form

● Period: Late Triassic
● Lived: 216.5–203.5 million years ago
● Size: up to 10 ft. (3m) long; 66 lb. (30kg)

Coelophysis

Tyrannosaurus rex
■ Meat Crunchers

✳ A towering terror with tiny arms and a bone-crunching bite
✳ With a long stride, T. rex could run at around 25 mph (40km/h)
✳ This meanie tyrannized western North America

Rooaaaarrrrr! You should be shakin' in your boots and quakin' at the thought of me, Tyrant King of dinosaurs. Trust me, if it walks, it's dinner—I'll even eat my own kind.

I'm a seek-and-destroy powerhouse. My forward-pointing peepers give me hawk-eyed vision, and whopping smell centers let me sniff out fresh meat and carrion over great distances. Despite my weight, I can be surprisingly light on my feet, allowing me to sneak up on my prey if I want to. My massive skull is equppied with flesh-shredding, saw-edged teeth, while powerful muscles in my neck help me pull and tear an animal to pieces once I've sunk my slashing gnashers in. You can see how well built I am, and yet my puny front limbs seem like a joke. Honestly, I can barely scratch my chin. Go on, laugh—I dare you!

● Discovered: 1902 (Montana)
● Pronunciation: tie-ran-oh-sore-us rex
● Name means: tyrant lizard king
● Period: Late Cretaceous
● Lived: 67–65 million years ago
● Size: up to 39 ft. (12m) long; 6.6 tons

Tyrannosaurus rex

Allosaurus

Meat Crunchers

- Ruthless killer with evil-looking ridge crests on the nose
- A common predator; possibly hunted in packs
- Fossils found in North America and Europe

Boy, oh boy, do I love surprises! Sadly, peaceful plant nibblers like Stegosaurus and Camptosaurus don't agree! I'm an ambush hunter. I creep up on other animals and then—boo!—I burst from cover and run them down.

Sleek and slim, I'm no lumberer. I can move it over short distances, running at 18–30 mph (30–50km/h). With a set of kitchen knives in my mouth—truly vicious saw-edged teeth—I can take out chunks of flesh while on the run. With my prey cornered, I jack my jaw wide open like a bear trap, sink my top row of pearly whites in, and chop like a hatchet. The damage this does to meat and muscle is staggering. And should anyone dare struggle, I hold them close in my strong arms until the wiggling stops . . . It's "Allo" from me and goodbye from them!

- Discovered: 1877 (Colorado)
- Pronunciation: al-oh-sore-us
- Name means: different lizard
- Period: Late Jurassic
- Lived: 155–145 million years ago
- Size: up to 26 ft. (8m) long; 2.2 tons

Allosaurus

Oviraptor
■ Meat Crunchers

☀ This little critter is an egg-snatching Mongolian mystery
☀ A toothless wonder with feathered arms but no wings
☀ Known from just one official fossil, found in the Gobi Desert

Polly want a cracker? Kwawk! I'm a prehistoric Polly, a dinosaur with a parrot beak. Some scientists think I'm more bird than dino, but I can assure you—I'm no turkey!

When my bones were found on top of a nest full of eggs, dino diggers figured I had been caught stealing, and they named me "egg thief." But the "yolk" was on them—they were my own waiting to hatch! I don't have any teeth, so it might seem odd that I'm a meat eater, and I have baffled scientists in the past. However, recent discoveries have revealed more about my eating habits—that I eat plants as well as tasty sauropodlet snacks, for example, which makes me something of an omnivore. My short, powerful beak can also be pretty handy for cracking open a few eggs! I like 'em fresh in the morning!

● Discovered: 1923 (Mongolia)
● Pronunciation: oh-vee-rap-tor
● Name means: egg thief

● Period: Late Cretaceous
● Lived: 75 million years ago
● Size: up to 6.5 ft. (2m) long; 55 lb. (25kg)

Oviraptor

Spinosaurus
■ Meat Crunchers

✳ Sail-backed dino with a crocodile face and fishy breath
✳ The last and largest of the fish-eating dinosaurs (piscivores)
✳ Hung out in the forest swamps of North Africa

I am the Cretaceous colossus, the biggest killer to stomp around on dry land. T. rex? Why, that puny fellow wouldn't even dare look me in the eye!

I can hunt down and tear apart any animal, sure, but it's fish I really love—gimme bus-size sawfish. My long snout has nostrils placed high up, allowing me to trail my pressure-sensitive nose in the water. I can literally feel my prey approaching and strike without seeing it. Instead of the jagged-edged teeth of other Meat Crunchers, mine are smooth and bullet shaped—ideal for stabbing and grabbing. Three razor-sharp claws on my hands do the rest! I am the top predator in these climes, but my position is fragile. Rising sea levels will eventually wipe out the swamplands where I live and I'll be hung out to dry!

● Discovered: 1912 (Egypt)
● Pronunciation: spine-oh-sore-us
● Name means: thorn lizard

● Period: Early/Late Cretaceous
● Lived: 112–97 million years ago
● Size: up to 50 ft. (14m) long; 11 tons

Spinosaurus

Baryonyx
■ Meat Crunchers

☀ Crocodile-snouted fish guzzler and relative of Spinosaurus
☀ Had a massive hooked claw on each hand
☀ This piscivore hunted in rivers in western Europe

I have a smile you won't easily forget! My mouth bristles with small serrated teeth—96 in all. That's twice as many as T. rex and three times as many as you. Say cheese!

Like Spinosaurus, I'm a fish eater, and I like to hang out along riverbanks and marshes. My slender snout stretches all the way to a delicate thin tip with a scooped end. My conical teeth have very fine sawlike edges—just the thing for snagging passing fishies and holding onto their wiggling bodies. Snappy! I'm also equipped with my very own gaffs (that's fish hooks to you), two 1.6-ft. (0.5-m) long hooked claws that make landing large fish a cinch. If you go to Alaska today, you'll see grizzly bears using the same method to spear salmon in the rapids. With claws like these, fish "bearly" stand a chance. Ha!

- Discovered: 1983 (Surrey, U.K.)
- Pronunciation: bare-ee-on-iks
- Name means: heavy claw
- Period: Early Cretaceous
- Lived: 130–125 million years ago
- Size: up to 31 ft. (9.5m) long; 2.8 tons

Baryonyx

Deinonychus
■ Meat Crunchers

✳ Brainy birdlike dinosaur that may have had feathers
✳ Nimble and lightly built; used its tail for balance
✳ This relative of Velociraptor lived in western North America

Speedy and agile, I have grasping fingers with long, curving claws. My mouth is full of sharp slashing teeth, designed to rip out chunks of flesh. Think that's scary? Well, think again. See the sickle-shaped second toe of each foot? Those are my daggers of death. Held off the ground when I run, they come down like blades when I leap onto my prey, gouging, tearing, and mangling. Shudder!

Deinonychus

● Discovered: 1964 (Montana)
● Pronunciation: die-non-ik-us
● Name means: terrible claw

● Period: Early Cretaceous
● Lived: 115–108 million years ago
● Size: up to 11.5 ft. (3.5m) long; 132 lb. (60kg)

Velociraptor
Meat Crunchers ■

☀ A big-brained, turkey-sized scavenger
☀ Fossilized in mortal combat with herbivore Protoceratops
☀ This violent critter roamed the wilds of Mongolia in Asia

Velociraptor

With my narrow head and long, feathered forelimbs, I am a curious-looking beast, I know. But looks aren't everything! The ultimate dino villain, I'm bloodthirsty and out for the kill. I have a mean-grip jaw, killer claws, and a tendency to go for the jugular. Speed is always of the essence, and my stiff tail stops me from teetering when in hot pursuit of a tasty snack.

● Discovered: 1923 (Mongolia)
● Pronunciation: vel-oss-ee-rap-tor
● Name means: speedy thief

● Period: Late Cretaceous
● Lived: 75–71 million years ago
● Size: up to 8 ft. (2.5m) long; 55 lb. (25kg)

Chapter 3
High-fliers

Strap on your flying goggles and prepare to take to the air with this brood of blue-sky riders. Aviation enthusiasts one and all, the High-fliers are recognized as the world's first flying vertebrates (animals with backbones to you). Not all of these critters were dinosaurs. Pterodactylus and Quetzalcoatlus were specialist reptiles with hollow bones and large brains to control their flight. Members of the dromeosaur family of dinosaurs, Rahonavis and Microraptor can claim to be true ancestors of the birds we see today. They were the first to grow feathers for show, for staying warm, and even for flight.

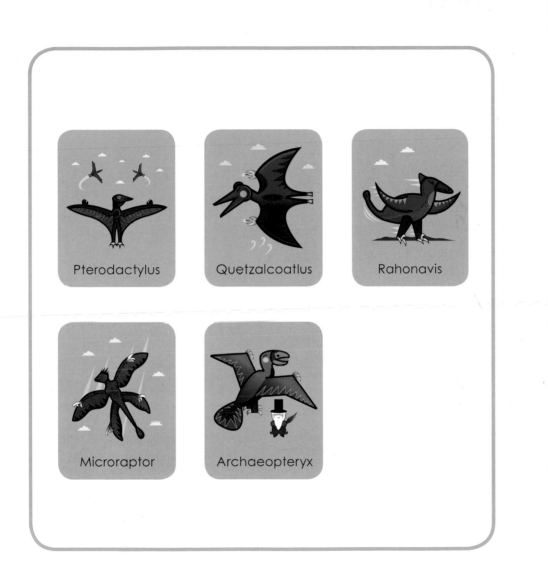

Pterodactylus

Quetzalcoatlus

Rahonavis

Microraptor

Archaeopteryx

Pterodactylus
■ High-fliers

* Furry flying reptile with a colored crest and pouched throat
* Armed with clawed fingers, a pointed beak, and sharp teeth
* This nondino has left its traces across Europe

A-duckin' and a-divin', a-skimmin' and a-bobbin', I love to fly the Jurassic skies. Each of my leathery wings hangs from an incredibly long fourth finger and stretches all the way to the ankle. I'm an airborne wonder. Zoom!

Some people think I am a dinosaur, but actually I'm a very close relative. My turbocharged breast muscles provide all a guy needs for powering flight, sometimes over long distances. My sharp little brain is capable of calculating fantastic tucks and bends, and a short tail allows me to make some stunning in-flight maneuvers. But I don't always have my head in the clouds. Nope, when it comes to food, you'll see me wading along the shore looking for crustaceans and mollusks. Armed with pin-sharp teeth, resistance is futile. Crunch!

- Discovered: 1780 (Germany)
- Pronunciation: ter-oh-dak-til-us
- Name means: winged finger
- Period: Late Jurassic
- Lived: 150–148 million years ago
- Size: 5 ft. (1.5m) wingspan; 10 lb. (4.5kg)

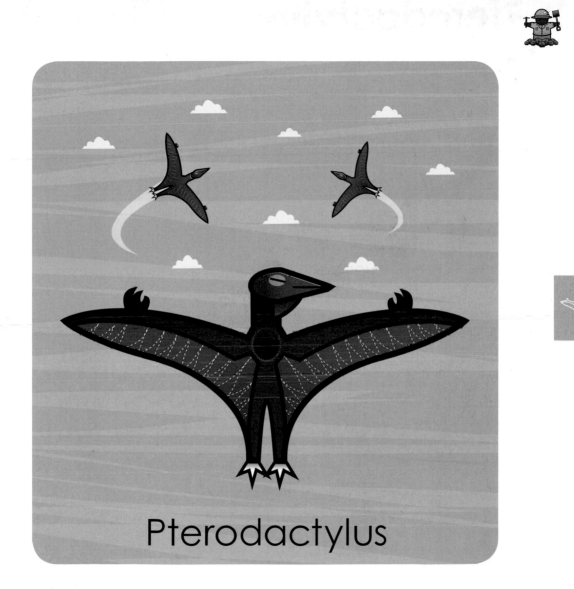

Pterodactylus

Quetzalcoatlus
■ High-fliers

✳ Cruising bruiser with a wingspan the size of a light aircraft
✳ The largest flying beast ever to have existed on Earth
✳ This terror of the skies inhabited North America

I'm an easy rider. With very little effort, I catch rising warm air under my leathery folds of skin to rise up, up, up where I can survey vast areas of the plains. Soaring high up above Earth, I use my impressive wings to keep me afloat and my beady eyes peeled for juicy snacks.

Everything about me is huge. It would take a champion long jumper to leap from one end of my head to the other. Fully opened, my wings stretch wider than a tennis court and are suspended from a fourth finger that could match the height of a soccer goalpost. When I land, I stand almost as tall as a giraffe. Stomping around on all fours, I hunt small reptiles and sauropodlets, bringing my huge pointed beak stabbing down on them. I also like to jab around in rotting carcasses. Finders, keepers!

● Discovered: 1972 (Texas)
● Pronunciation: kwet-zal-co-at-lus
● Name means: feathered serpent

● Period: Late Cretaceous
● Lived: 68–65.5 million years ago
● Size: 39 ft. (12m) wingspan; 55 lb. (250kg)

Quetzalcoatlus

Rahonavis
■ High-fliers

✸ Raven-sized dinobird and relative of the dromeosaurs
✸ Like all dromeosaurs, this dino had a raised sickle claw
✸ Hailed from the African island of Madagascar

I'm a small feathered fella, a speedy runner, and a darting predator. At some point in time, millions of years ago, modern birds evolved from dinos just like me. Experts think I might have taken to the skies, too. Well, look at my long, muscly arms. Why shouldn't they support wings that I can flap to get me airborne? Hence my reputation, I say, as a menace from the clouds.

Rahonavis

● Discovered: 1995 (Madagascar)
● Pronunciation: rah-hoo-nay-vis
● Name means: menace bird

● Period: Late Cretaceous
● Lived: 70 million years ago
● Size: up to 28 in. (70cm) long; 2 lb. (1kg)

Microraptor

High-fliers ■

☀ Mini gliding dinobird with four wings and a long tail
☀ A poor groundrunner, this critter lived in trees
☀ Most common dromeosaur fossil, many with plumage

Microraptor

Hey! Up here! Watch me skitter around in the trees, digging my claws in for the climb. Admiring my fabulous feathers? You should be, 'cause these fancy things are not for warmth or colorful display. No, I use these bad boys for flight while my long stabilizing tail guides my descent. Swooping and gliding back down to Earth, you could say I'm a dinosoar!

● Discovered: 2003 (China)
● Pronunciation: mike-row-rap-tor
● Name means: small thief

● Period: Early Cretaceous
● Lived: 120 million years ago
● Size: up to 16 in. (40cm) long; 2 lb. (1kg)

Archaeopteryx
■ High-fliers

❋ This dinobird's discovery supported the theory of evolution
❋ One of the earliest birds, but still counted as a dinosaur
❋ This handsome beast inhabited Germany

I don't like to boast, but my discovery more than 150 years ago takes some beating, I can tell you. At the time, I could claim to be the world's first-ever bird. Just imagine! Even though this is now disputed, my significance for the evolution of birds from dinosaurs is no less diminished.

You see, I'm definitely a dino: like my dromeosaur relatives, I have small biting teeth in my beak, clawed fingers in each wing, a cocked "killing claw," and a long bony tail. But (and it's a big but) like modern birds, I also have flight-ready feathers. Don't believe me? Look at my exquisite fossils! These glorious impressions made in the mud were found just two years after Charles Darwin published his theories on evolution. I helped prove that he really had discovered something. Boy, he must have loved me!

- Discovered: 1861 (Germany)
- Pronunciation: ark-ee-op-ter-iks
- Name means: ancient wing
- Period: Late Jurassic
- Lived: 150–148.5 million years ago
- Size: up to 20 in. (50cm) long; 2 lb. (1kg)

Archaeopteryx

Chapter 4
Water Lovers

Here's a fine bunch of scary sea monsters, huge predatory beasts that prowled the world's oceans with menace. Around at the same time as the dinos that roamed the land, these fearsome Water Lovers actually belonged to a group of marine reptiles. Like modern oceangoing mammals—whales, dolphins, and porpoises—they were air breathers, which means they needed to surface from time to time. These days, the only surviving marine reptiles are turtles, snakes, iguanas, and crocodiles . . . and none are as monstrous as this group were! Are you ready to take the plunge?

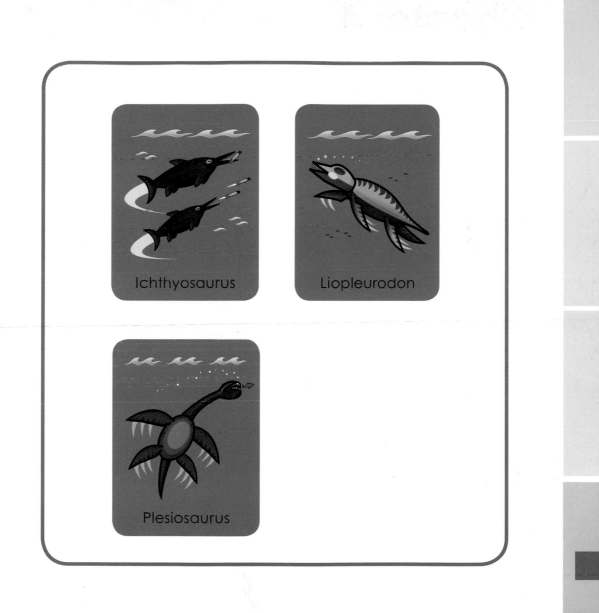

Ichthyosaurus

Liopleurodon

Plesiosaurus

Ichthyosaurus
■ Water Lovers

✷ Shark-tailed, tuna-shaped marine reptile
✷ Warm-blooded; gave birth to live young in the water
✷ This swift swimmer has left its mark in Europe

Whoosh! Streamlined and slick, I'm built for sheer speed in the water. See me flashing past, and I bet you'd be forced to look twice. You might think that I'm a huge tuna, but I'm no fish—I'm reptile to the bone!

I power myself along using my tail, graciously sweeping it from side to side like a shark. I have stiff fins that help me maneuver, twist, and tumble in the water. And I tuck them in tight to my body when I need a burst of speed. My top-mounted dorsal fin gives me stability as I swim and a nice "ride" in the water. I am an air breather, like a dolphin, and my big eyes show that I am an active chaser of fish. I have lovely pointed teeth—perfect for cracking open shellfish ammonites or crunchy, squiddy belemnites. Mmm, nice with a squeeze of lemon!

● Discovered: 1811 (U.K.)
● Pronunciation: ick-thee-oh-sore-us
● Name means: fish lizard

● Period: Late Triassic/Early Jurassic
● Lived: 200–185 million years ago
● Size: up to 6.5 ft. (2m) long; 198 lb. (90kg)

Ichthyosaurus

Liopleurodon
■ Water Lovers

✳ Gigantic, powerfully built short-necked shark eater
✳ Predator of the Jurassic seas; Earth's largest carnivore . . . ever
✳ Fossils of this massive beast have been found in Europe

Behold, the top terror of the Jurassic seas, master of the largest jaws this planet has ever seen! A monster mega predator, I'll have large fry for supper. My huge teeth make short work of bone and gristle. Chomp!

Considered antisocial and violent, when I say "come over for dinner," it's not exactly a chat over a light bite that I'm after. I cruise under the water, moving slowly and menacingly. I have a large, compact head and an impressively muscular body and tail. Flapping my front and back fins out of time with each other, what I lack in grace, I make up for in power. I'm an ambush killer— my giant flippers give me blistering acceleration on demand. I hunt using my sharp sense of smell, sweeping my head from side to side, silently searching. Sniff, sniff!

- Discovered: 1873 (France)
- Pronunciation: lie-oh-plew-roh-don
- Name means: smooth-sided teeth
- Period: Mid/Late Jurassic
- Lived: 162–150 million years ago
- Size: up to 49 ft. (15m); 22 tons

Liopleurodon

Plesiosaurus
■ Water Lovers

✳ Marine reptile with a short tail, a long neck, and four flippers
✳ Able to swim faster than an Olympic swimmer
✳ This underwater wonder inhabited European waters

Hello there! With my toothy grin and snappy style, I'm one happy swimmer—a fish-chasin', air-breathin', fully oceangoin' reptile. Very "plesio" to meet you!

My body is short, broad, and well muscled. They say I look like a snake threaded through a turtle shell, but that's silly 'cause I don't even have a shell! It's true that my neck is long, but it's not that flexible. Instead, it's the expert way in which I operate my flippers that gives me the skill required for such fine swimming. I move nothing like a turtle, which uses only its front flippers for propulsion. No, I use all four: first the front pair, then the back. With a little gentle flapping, I glide through the water in pursuit of deliciously fishy food. I might even graze the ocean floor for a clam or snail. I'm a refined sort of guy, you know!

● Discovered: 1823 (U.K.)
● Pronunciation: plee-see-oh-sore-us
● Name means: ribbon lizard

● Period: Early Jurassic
● Lived: 199–176 million years ago
● Size: up to 11.5 ft. (3.5m); 1,100 lb. (500kg)

Plesiosaurus

Index

Character entries are **bold**

LMN

Liopleurodon **56**
Maiasaura **12**
meat eaters, see
  carnivores
Microraptor 42, **49**
necks 10, 14 , 21, 22, 30,
  56, 58, 63, 64
nests 12, 34, 62

O

omnivores 34, 63
ornithiscians 4, 63
Oviraptor **34**
Owen, Richard 4

PQ

Pachycephalosaurus **21**
pack hunters 28, 32
Parasaurolophus **18**
piscivores 36, 38, 44, 54, 56,
  58, 62, 63
plant eaters, see herbivores
Plesiosaurus **58**
Protoceratops 41
Pterodactylus 42, **44**
Quetzalcoatlus 42, **46**

RS

Rahonavis 42, **48**
reptiles 42, 44, 46, 52, 54,
  58, 62, 63, 64
saurischians 4, 64
sauropods 34, 46, 64
snouts 36, 38
Spinosaurus **36**, 38
Stegosaurus **16**, 32

T

tails 10, 16, 20, 22, 40, 41, 44,
  49, 50, 54, 56, 58, 64
tail spikes 6, 16, 64
teeth 4, 8, 12, 18, 21, 22, 24,
  26, 30, 32, 34, 36, 38, 40, 44,
  50, 54, 56, 58, 62, 63, 64
theropods 28, 64
Triassic period 28, 54, 64
Triceratops **14**
Tyrannosaurus rex 4, 14, **30**,
  36, 38, 64

VW

Velociraptor 40, **41**
wings 44, 46, 48, 49, 50

Glossary

Ammonite Belongs to an extinct group of mollusks with spiral shells. Closely related to octopuses, squids, and cuttlefish but looks more like a modern nautilus. Died out at the same time as dinosaurs.

Battery (dental) A large block of fused teeth that often has as many as five individual teeth stacked on top of each other in every position. Useful for grinding and crushing plants and also seen in modern elephants.

Belemnite An extinct squidlike mollusk with a bullet-shaped, hard internal skeleton. Became extinct around the same time as dinosaurs.

Bipedal Walking on two legs.

Carnivore A meat-eating animal.

Carrion The body of a dead animal, also known as a "carcass." It is a food source for other animals.

Ceratopsian A herbivorous, quadrupedal beaked dinosaur of the Cretaceous period.

Communal nesting Often seen in ceratopsian dinosaurs, as well as modern reptiles and birds, where groups of mothers lay their eggs in the same location, most likely for protection against predators. Fossilized sites give clues to dinosaur behavior.

Crest A ridge, whirl, or tube of bone on top of the head. Hadrosaur crests were often hollow and may have been used to make sounds.

Cretaceous A geological period following the Jurassic and running from 145 to 65 million years ago. During this period, the climate was warm and the sea level high. This was the last age of dinosaurs.

Dromeosaur A carnivorous dinosaur, related to birds.

Fossil The remains of a prehistoric creature that has been preserved as a mold or cast in rock.

Frill Extra skin jutting out from the head, often supported by bone in ceratopsian dinosaurs.

Herbivore A plant-eating animal.

Hide The skin of a large animal, often thick and tough.

Jugular A large vein in the neck of an animal.

Jurassic A geological period following the Triassic and running from 200 to 145 million years ago. The climate was wetter than the Triassic, with dinosaurs ruling the land, marine reptiles in the oceans, and flying reptiles in the skies.

Omnivore An animal that eats both plants and meat.

Ornithiscian A plant-eating dinosaur with hipbones that resemble those of modern birds (often called a bird-hipped dinosaur).

Peg tooth A simple, slightly tapered tooth formation.

Piscivore A fish-eating animal.

Plumage The layer of feathers covering an animal.

Predator A hunting animal that feeds on other animals.

Prey An animal that is hunted and killed for food.

Glossary

Reptile A cold-blooded vertebrate animal with dry, scaly skin that lays eggs on land. Modern reptiles include snakes, lizards, crocodiles, turtles, and tortoises.

Saurischian A dinosaur with hipbones that resemble those of modern reptiles (often called a lizard-hipped dinosaur). All carnivorous dinosaurs (theropods) were saurischians, as well as plant-eating sauropods.

Sauropod An extremely large saurischian, plant-eating dinosaur with a long neck, long tail, and small head. It first appeared in the Late Triassic period.

Serrated Describes jagged-edged teeth and claws.

Sickle claw A large, curving hook claw seen in the dromeosaurid family, such as Deinonychus.

Thagomizer The spike-studded tail defense used by stegosaurs (usually with four to ten spikes).

Theropod A bipedal carnivorous dinosaur with three-toed feet that appeared in the Late Triassic period. Includes many famous meat eaters, such as Tyrannosaurus rex.

Ton A unit of mass equal to 2,000 pounds (907kg).

Triassic A geological period following the Permian and running from 250 to 200 million years ago. The period was hot and dry and witnessed the rise and dominance of dinosaurs.